TAMAR

C000244325

Cognitive behavioral

Therapy

A BEGINNERS GUIDE TO OVERCOME
ANXIETY, INSOMNIA & DEPRESSION, BREAK
NEGATIVE THOUGHT PATTERNS AND
MAINTAIN MINDFULNESS WITH THE BEST CBT
TECHNIQUES

TABLE OF CONTENTS

CHAPTER 1:

What Is Cognitive Behavioral Therapy?

Think of yourself as a slate that has so many words, images, and texts scribbled over it in a way that makes it impossible to make sense of anything. You cannot tell where one text starts and where the other ends, but you are sure that they are all linked together in a way, but you just can't figure out how. If you were confronted with such a board, you would be saddened by its current state. It is not like a puzzle that you already have a clear picture of what the end product is meant to be. To make sense of this slate, you would have to get to the root word or foundational phrase. When you find that foundation, you may have to erase individual words and replace them with suitable alternatives; in sum, it is only as you piece each new word that you begin to see a semblance of normalcy. This process is what cognitive-behavioral therapy encompasses.

When you find yourself acting, thinking, and speaking in ways that you ought not to due to excessive anger, crippling anxiety, overwhelming depression, and an upsurge of negative words, it would be impossible for life to make sense. This is because everything you do would be filtered through these emotions. It would seem as though everyone in the entire world is out to get you. Every step you take would seem to be steeped heavily in led. Little events spark up rage in you so volatile that it would seem you are carrying a little hurricane on the inside of you that is spinning everything out of control and destroying everything in its path. And it doesn't matter if it is raining outside or the sun is shining so bright since you have your thunderstorm complete with thick dark clouds and heavy showers that are programmed to flush out any happy thought or feeling. No wonder you feel the way you do. Your slate is wholly messed up.

With Cognitive Behavioral Therapy (CBT), you start to understand why you feel the way you do. It is only in answering why you can determine how you can tip the scales in your favor. You did not wake up overnight and began to feel the way you do. Even if your condition is inherited, you have established several behavioral patterns over time that cause these conditions to set in. With Cognitive Behavioral Therapy, you can identify those behavioral patterns and offset their influence by deliberately replacing them with better behavioral practices that are more suitable. However, it has also been known to treat long-term ailments like irritable bowel syndrome, controlled by better eating behavior.

However, it is essential to note that Cognitive Behavioral Therapy is not designed as a curative measure. Far from it. Instead, it helps you cope better with those conditions by effectively helping you take control of your emotions. For CBT to work, you will require the following in equal measure:

- Consistency
- Diligence
- Willingness
- Honesty

The goal is to help you establish new behaviors to manage anger, anxiety, depression, and negative thoughts. They say that it takes 21 days to develop a new habit. But that is not the reason we (you and I) are working with 21 days.

Simultaneously, specific behavioral elements can be introduced to reverse the experience and bring you to a place where you can better cope with whatever is happening.

These daily exercises are straightforward, but the effect is powerful. Some must be conducted repeatedly to affect. However, if done right, you can notice a significant difference from the first try. Others must be combined in specific scenarios for maximum impact, and I have carefully pointed those out as well. To get the desired results, you must be deliberate in taking each action. It also helps to curate your experience post the action. This would help you put things in perspective and give you some insight into problematic areas. There is so much going on in your life right now, and none of it is probably making sense.

We (you and I) are using Cognitive Behavioral Therapy to retrace your steps, realign your behavior with the emotional results you are hoping to achieve, and generally bring you to a place where you are emotionally balanced and content in who you are experiences you have in life. Because let's face it, life will always have those terrible and unfair incidents happen to us even though we are not quite deserving of those situations. But we don't have to let those incidences define us. When we root ourselves in our true identity, we will not be quickly phased by what happens outside. There will be moments when you will slip. And that fall will discourage you from going forward. A momentary slip is not the end of the world. This is what makes you human. The part that makes you extraordinary is choosing to get up from that fall, but the pieces that were broken apart and resolved to be stronger for it. You are made of more, and over 21 days, you will discover just how amazing you are!

CHAPTER 2:

Cognitive Behavioral Therapy for Depression

Restructuring

C hallenging your thoughts is going to be the most powerful tool. Like anxiety, look for the factual data and analytics of a situation to put some logic into your thoughts. When we can look at the factual data that can be numerically measured, it can be harder to have depressive thoughts about our situation. It is not about just being grateful for what you have but instead looking at the positive things in your life rather than emphasizing the negative.

Always ask yourself real questions and test the evidence that you have for a particular prediction. This isn't going to make you feel better right at that moment.

However, if you start this combative of automatic thoughts right now, it will get better every day. You have to be patient and willing to put that time in.

Combating Thoughts

Now that you have some Cognitive Behavioral Therapy tools, you have to look at yourself as a warrior fighting against the cognitive distortions. You are holding a shield, and you have to fight off all the distortions your mind is throwing at you. Sometimes, they might still slip pass, but it is up to you to keep them from destroying you. It might seem impossible, but you should always combat your negative thoughts as they come toward you. Humans are obsessed with labels. Not just ones that come from a label maker, but more general ones, like good/bad, fat/skinny, ugly/pretty, useful/useless, smart/stupid. We like to put things into one category, especially if you are someone with depressive tendencies and polarized thinking.

Look at the Root

When using CBT, you want to go back to that time a specific event took place and think about why that event or comment affected you so. Sometimes, when a person states something related to our insecurities, it can be a form of validation, good or bad. If you think you are not intelligent and someone makes a small joke about your smartness level, it can cut pretty deep, even though it wasn't meant to be hurtful at all. This is because it is an unspoken validation from the other person that our deepest and darkest thoughts are right, even though that wasn't the other person's intention. Remember that small instances are just that. Though they might have become defining moments, they don't have to anymore. Most of the time, if you ask a person about certain small instances that stick with you, they end up not even remembering that they said that in the first place!

Journaling

Expressing your feelings is an incredibly effective way to overcome your mental illnesses. Holding things in can be like a plastic bag or even a boat. If you put too much in, it is going to sink or break. The same can be said with your mind. If you are not adequately healthily expressing your feelings, it will take a toll on your mental and physical health.

Journaling is entirely subjective. Everyone's mind is different, and that means their journal should be as well. What you decide to put in your journal is up to you. The main idea is that it should be an expression of your emotions, recording of your different feelings, and a go-to for helpful reminders or a guide to overcoming anxiety and depressive thoughts. You can go back and look at to see different information to help you continue in your recovery.

Quantitative Data

Some people aren't creative or have trouble expressing their emotions, and that's completely fine. They might not be able to write full entries. Writing might be awful to you, and the sound of it alone gives you anxiety. That's completely fine.

Look at your journal for answers that aren't always easily identifiable. Even if you are creative, this method of journaling can still help as well. You could aim to implement both, but it is up to you to figure out what works best with managing your depression at the end of the day.

Writing Letters

Sometimes, we stay quiet in situations that require us to speak up because we don't know how to process our emotions. One way to change this is to write letters. This can be a part of your journal, or it can be completely separate. Maybe you write one to yourself at five years old, and one when you are fifty. Write a letter to yourself yesterday, angry that you weren't able to get as much work done as you hoped. Write one to your ten-year-old self, letting that kid know that it was OK they didn't make the volleyball team or that it wasn't their fault their parents fought all the time.

Write one to yourself in the future. Tell yourself how much you have thought about them and how you hope they are doing well. By doing this, you are expressing emotions that you have kept inside. Other times, you might want to write letters to other people. Maybe you are angry, so you write down everything you hate about them. While it might be hard to go through those feelings, it can be incredibly therapeutic to get your thoughts out.

Unraveling

When unraveling, you have to make sure that you are looking at the cause and effect of different cognitive distortions. One end will be the cause, and the other end will be the effect. When you have it all raveled together, it can be hard to process. When things are laid out correctly, you will see easier the things that upset or frustrated you.

What you have to unravel is going to be different for everyone, but some necessary steps can help you do this:

- Identify the symptom of anxiety. What is it that has made you decide to use CBT?

- Pick out what cognitive distortion might have led to your symptoms. Do you often deflect? How are you framing the issue? Are there moments of catastrophizing?

- Reflect on the issue and see the ways they've grown roots and spread. How have they affected other parts of your life?

- Look to your past to see what might have caused the issue in the first place. Was there a specific trauma, or did you experience prolonged abuse?

- Come up with a solution for resolving this issue. Which method of CBT is going to be the most useful for you to overcome it? Sometimes, unraveling will be enough in itself, but you have to use multiple methods other times.

This is just a straightforward method of unraveling. It starts with the issue and ends with a solution. Though it looks easy, it won't always be that simple to carry out step five, the recovery methods. However, looking at it in these simple steps can help ensure that you are logically looking at your anxiety and depression.

CHAPTER 3:

Cognitive Behavioral Therapy for Insomnia

Insomnia

Insomnia is a sleep disorder that makes it difficult for a person to fall asleep or stay asleep and, in some cases, causes you to wake up early and be unable to fall back to sleep. Because of a lack of proper sleep, a person usually feels tired after waking up. Insomnia disorder is terrible because it saps out your energy, affects your mood and health, and your work performance.

Enough sleep varies from one individual to another, but adults' recommended sleep is seven to eight hours of sleep each night.

At a certain point in most adult's lives, a person may experience acute insomnia that can last for several days or weeks. However, some people suffer from prolonged periods of chronic insomnia. This type of insomnia may be associated with other conditions that need medical attention.

With simple daily habits, one can overcome insomnia and go back to enjoying healthy sleep patterns. How does a person know they have insomnia? Insomnia has various distinct symptoms. These may include:

- Finding it difficult to fall asleep during bedtime
- Losing sleep in the halfway through the night
- Getting up very early
- I am feeling tired even after a night's sleep.
- I am feeling tired during the day and sleepy.
- Being irritable, anxious, and depressed
- Finding it hard to be attentive, focused on assignments, or remembering.
- Having a higher rate of mistakes and accidents
- I am always worried about sleep.

When Should One See a Doctor?

If the lack of sleep is so severe that you find it hard to function in your day to day activities, seeing a doctor is advisable. The doctor should work with you to identify the cause of insomnia and develop various treatment options. In case the doctor feels that you are suffering from a sleep disorder, he may recommend you see a sleep specialist.

How Age Relates to Insomnia?

Insomnia can be directly related to one's age. The older a person gets, the more they experience insomnia. When a person gets older, they experience:

- Your sleep pattern changes — as a person ages, sleep becomes less. Slight noise or other changes in one's environment can cause a person to wake up frequently. Age causes the internal clock to advance, making one tired earlier at night and waking up even earlier. Regardless, it is healthy to have the same amount of sleep when older, just like a younger person.

- If you are less active during the day, changes in what you do may take an afternoon nap. This, in the end, will interfere with your sleep at night.

- Change in health — if a person experiences chronic pain from conditions like arthritis or back pains, they may have challenges sleeping. Other conditions, like anxiety or depression, also interfere with sleep. Other medical issues may cause frequent urinating at night, such as bladder problems, diabetes, among others. Restless leg syndrome and sleep apnea are also other conditions that interrupt sleep patterns.

- Prescription drugs — older people use more prescription medicines than younger people do. This increases the chance of developing chronic insomnia.

Insomnia can affect children and teenagers, as well. However, most of the causes at this age is due to their irregular patterns in their sleep schedules. Lack of sleep can also be associated with some risks in specific individuals.

The Risk of Suffering from Insomnia Is more significant if:

- The individual is a woman. Shifts in the hormones during the menstrual cycle or menopause play a significant role. When a woman is going through menopause, they experience hot flashes and night sweats that will interrupt sleep. Pregnant mothers also experience insomnia due to hormonal changes.

- If you are over the age of 60, then your chances of suffering from insomnia are high. As you age, you experience changes in health, increasing the risk of insomnia.

- If you are experiencing a mental health disorder or a physical health condition, you are at a greater risk of developing insomnia.

- Stress is another condition that increases insomnia. When a person is undergoing stressful situations, they may have temporary insomnia. However, prolonged periods of stress may also result in chronic insomnia in many individuals.

- Lack of regular schedule is another contributor to insomnia. A person that often travels across different time zones or works with various shifts is likely to experience insomnia.

Insomnia Complications

Just like having a healthy diet is essential, having healthy sleep patterns is also essential and regular. Regardless of the reasons causing your lack of sleep, insomnia can physically and mentally affect you negatively. Individuals with insomnia have a lower quality of life as compared to individuals that enjoy good sleeping habits.

Various complications associated with insomnia include:

- Poor performance at work or school
- Decreased reaction time on the road that may result in higher risks of accidents
- Mental health disorders like anxiety, substance abuse, and depression
- Higher risk of long-term diseases such as heart diseases.

Practical Strategies that Will Help You Sleep better

Developing good sleep habits can help prevent insomnia and cause a person to enjoy a sound sleep. Some practical things you can do to improve your sleep will include:

- Be consistent in your bed and wake time even during the weekends.

- Be active. Regular physical activity will aid in promoting good night sleep.

- Check your medications if one of the side effects is lack of sleep. If so, speak to your doctor to switch the medicine.

- Try and avoid daytime naps, and if you feel you must, limit the duration.

- Limit or avoid the use of nicotine, alcohol, or caffeine entirely.

- Avoid taking huge meals before bedtime and taking of sugary beverages.

- Don't use your bedroom as a work station or a place for entertainment. Use it only for the intended purpose.

Come up with a relaxing bedtime ritual, like taking a warm shower, listening to soft music in low volume, or reading.

CHAPTER 4:

Cognitive Behavioral Therapy for Anxiety

S trong emotions arise before thoughts related to them are fully formed, not afterward, as it likely appears when you look back on an incredibly emotional incident. As such, you will often find that it is easier–and more effective–to change how you feel about a situation than what you think about a situation. As such, if you want to use CBT to help your anxiety, then the following exercises are a great way to work on calming your feelings directly:

Focus on how Your Feelings Change

When working with CBT, it can be easy to get so focused on the way your feelings are currently aligned that it can be easy to forget that feelings are fluid, which means they are always open to change, even after you have already put in the effort to work on them for another specific reason. Likewise, just because you spend a month or more working on your feelings of anxiety, it doesn't mean that you aren't still going to get a little anxious now and again. Instead, it is essential to take the new anxiety in your stride and see how severe it ends up being before you get too stressed out about it, possibly causing yourself far more mental strife than you would have had you just taken the small amount of anxiety in your stride in the first place.

You may also find it helpful to verbally acknowledge how you feel in the moment and how you expect those feelings to change once the anxiety has passed. For example, you might say, "Currently, I felt a little anxious, which is natural given the situation.

When the feeling passes, I anticipate feeling clear-headed and calm once more."

Additionally, you may find it helpful to keep a close eye out for the first signs that the feeling is passing, and the anticipated change is about to begin. Not only will focusing on the anxiety being over actually make the end come on sooner, but it will also stop you from reacting poorly to the anxiety at the moment. Feelings always shift, and keeping this fact in mind may be enough to push things in the right direction.

Act Normally

While Generalized Anxiety Disorder is considered a mental illness, anxiety itself is a useful survival tool when doled out in moderation. It is only when things get out of hand that it goes from being helpful to harmful, sort of like an over-eager guard dog. The truth of the matter is that your anxiety response only kicks in because your body responds to the current situation as if there was a threat. Regardless of whether the threat is real, a perceived threat is enough to set off the response.

As such, one way to train your anxiety to be selective effectively is to give it the type of feedback it understands so that it knows it is not currently needed. Anxiety takes its cues from what you do along with a primary type of emotional pattern matching, which means that if you act as though everything is currently standard, then the anxiety will back off and calm down. As such, you will want to do things such as maintain an open body posture, breathe regularly, salivate, smile, and maintain a calm and measured tone of voice.

Suppose you can successfully adopt just one of these behaviors when you are feeling stressed. In that case, you can successfully alter your feedback enough that your fear response, directly from the sympathetic nervous system, receives a message that says everything is fine. One of the most common ways of mitigating an oncoming feeling of anxiety is to chew gum. If you don't have any gum handy, only miming the act of doing so is going to be enough to make you drool, convincing your body that nothing interesting is going on.

The reason that this is so effective is that you would never have the luxury of eating a delicious meal during times of severe crisis, which makes your body naturally assume that nothing that taking place is a legitimate threat. This, in turn, changes the feedback loop the body was expecting and causes the anxiety to retreat into the background. Just knowing that you have this quick trick in your back pocket can give you a boost of confidence that takes you past the point where your anxiety would trigger in the first place.

Remember, anxiety functions are based on the expectation of something catastrophic happening shortly. All you need to do is prove that this is not the case, and you will be fine.

Discover underlying Assumptions

As a general rule, if you feel anxious about a specific situation, then this is because you are afraid of some potential consequences that may come about as a result of whatever it is that is taking place. However, if you trace those fears back to their roots, you will often find that they aren't nearly as bad as you may have assumed, they would be when they were just a nebulous feeling of anxiety. For example, if you are anxious about attending a party, then looking inside to determine the consequence you are afraid of might reveal an internalized fear of meeting new people. Tracing that fear back, you might discover that it is based around the consequence of other people not liking you, which you are determined to avoid due to issues in your past.

However, if you trace the consequence of people not liking you, then you may find that it makes you upset because it reinforces existing feelings regarding your general likeability. Once you get to the ultimate consequence that is causing you anxiety, you can look at the problem critically and determine what you can do to solve the issue that you are avoiding. In this instance, reminding yourself of people who do like you is an excellent way to avoid the issues you are afraid of.

This exercise is also incredibly useful for those dealing with relationship issues, as they can clearly describe all of the fears, they have associated with the relationship falling apart. In the process, they will understand that things will continue as usual after the relationship falls apart and move on if the relationship is not intact.

Progressive Muscle Relaxation

Another useful technique in combating anxiety is known as progressive muscle relaxation. This exercise involves tensing and then relaxing parts of your body in order. This is because the body can't be both tense and relaxed at the same time. Thus, if you feel an anxiety attack coming on, a round of concentrated tense and release exercises can cut it off at the source. Progressive muscle relaxation exercises may be done routinely or before an anxiety-provoking event. Progressive muscle relaxation techniques may also be used to help people who are experiencing insomnia.

To get started, find a calm, quiet place that you can dedicate to the process for approximately 15 minutes. Start by taking five, slow, deep breaths to get yourself into the right mindset. You are going to want to apply muscle tension to a specific part of your body. This step is going to be the same regardless of the muscle group you are currently focusing on. Focus on the muscle group before taking another slow, deep breath and then squeezing the muscles as hard as you possibly can for approximately five seconds. The goal here is to feel the tension in your muscles as fully as possible, to the point that you feel a mild discomfort before you have finished.

Once you have finished tensing, rapidly relax the muscles you were focusing on. After five seconds of tensing, let all of the tightness flow out of your muscles, exhaling as you do so. The goal here is to feel the muscles become limp and loose as the tension flows out. It is crucial that you deliberately focus on the difference between the two states; this is the most crucial exercise. Remain in this state of relaxation for approximately 15 seconds before moving on to the other group of muscles.

CHAPTER 5:

Cognitive Behavioral Therapy for OCD and Intrusive Thoughts

I n recent times, OCD has become somewhat of a common term in everyday society. The word is often thrown around lightly as a tease to someone who likes things a certain way or feels the need to be orderly and tidy. Most of the people who do this, however, don't even know the first thing about OCD or how serious it is.

Obsessive-Compulsive Disorder (OCD) is a chronic mental condition affecting more than 2.2 million individuals in the United States. It is defined by distracting and disturbing thoughts, pictures, or impulses that often cause someone to participate in repetitive, ritualistic, or mental conduct. Understandably, those suffering from OCD feel a great deal of anxiety about their illness because they feel like they are slaves to their obsessions and compulsions. It can also make it difficult for a person to think about it.

Another challenge that a lot of OCD patients struggle with is overcoming their need to enact their obsessive thoughts into compulsions. OCD is driven by anxiety, and people with this disorder often wrongly believe that the only way to alleviate their anxiety is by giving in to their compulsions. While it does provide some relief, it's a maladaptive solution to a much more complex problem, as it can take away an individual's sense of control and free will over their lives.

In the early days of psychotherapy, OCD was one of the most prevalent mental disorders globally, but most psychologists didn't have the faintest clue on how to treat it. Many of them simply resorted to psychodynamic therapy, behavioral therapy, and antidepressants, even though it was proven to have little to no significant effect.

Fortunately, in 1966, psychologists discovered the first effective psychosocial intervention for OCD: exposure and ritual prevention (EX/RP).

EX/RP is a CBT technique that proved to be so successful in treating the disorder that it went on to inspire the development of other similar treatments, most of which with successful outcomes. Now, Cognitive-Behavioral Therapy (CBT) and its specialized techniques are considered the "golden standard" in treating OCD patients and alleviating their anxiety. It also helps them manage their obsessions and decrease their compulsions, which adds to better life quality.

So, if you're suffering from OCD and looking to CBT to help you manage your condition better and ease your troubles, then you've come to the right place. But first, let's go over the different kinds of obsessive thoughts and compulsions.

Among the most common obsessive thoughts include themes of:

- Orderliness and symmetry — People with this kind of OCD often worry about the neatness and tidiness of everything
- Contamination — This lead someone to fear being contaminated with germs and bacteria

- Rumination — This means imagining a mistake that one has done or might do

- Checking — This type of obsession leaves the person wondering if they've already turned off the lights, turned off the stove, locked the doors, etc.

- Dark Thoughts — This induces a fear of even thinking about "sinful" or evil things

- Violence — A person with these thoughts often fears harming others, even though he/she does not want or intend to

As for compulsive behaviors, among the essential kinds are:

- Skin-picking
- Hair-pulling
- Hoarding/collecting
- Repeated hand washing or cleaning
- Repeating particular words or phrases
- Performing certain tasks repeatedly
- Constant counting

As you can see, OCD can have many different subtypes and symptoms, depending on the individual's particular obsessions or compulsions. But more often than not, effective treatment for one type of OCD is sufficient for the rest as well. There is also the degree of the severity of OCD that needs to be put into consideration.

CHAPTER 6:

Using CBT to Beat Procrastination

S everal factors lead us to procrastinate. Once we understand these factors, we'll consider the many tools that CBT offers for breaking this habit.

Do You Have a Procrastination Problem?

People vary in their tendency to procrastinate and in the specific tasks they put off doing. Take some time to consider ways you might delay doing things you know you need to do. Do you find yourself in any of the following situations regularly due to procrastination?

- Realizing you didn't leave yourself enough time to finish a task by the deadline.
- Feeling inadequately prepared for meetings.
- Trying to force yourself to do a task.

- Being stressed about time as you rush to appointments.

- Trying to hide that you haven't been working on a task.

- Producing lower quality work than you're capable of.

- Telling yourself, "I'll take care of that sooner."

- Waiting to feel more inspired or motivated so you can do a task.

- Finding ways to waste time instead of doing what you need to do.

- Relying on last-minute pressure to complete a task.

Let's begin by considering why we procrastinate and then turn to ways to overcome it.

What Drives Procrastination?

We've all been there — a paper to write, an errand to run, a home project to start, or any number of other tasks we put off. Little good seems to come from these delays — for example, procrastination is associated with worse academic performance and more significant sickness. Nevertheless, we often struggle to take care of things in a timely way. The following factors contribute to our tendency to procrastinate:

- Fear that it will be unpleasant: When we think about doing a task, our minds often go automatically to the most unenjoyable parts. If we imagine cleaning the gutters, we think about wrestling with the ladder. When we consider writing a paper, we dwell on the struggle we'll have at times to express our ideas clearly.

- Negative reinforcement: Every time we put off a task, we think it will be unpleasant. We experience a feeling of relief. The brain interprets that relief as a reward, and we're more likely to repeat an action that led to reward. In this way, our procrastination is reinforced. Psychologists call it "negative reinforcement" because it comes about by taking away something seen as aversive. In contrast, positive reinforcement is when getting something we like strengthens a behavior — for example, receiving a paycheck reinforces our job's behavior. The negative reinforcement from avoiding a task can be tough to overcome.

- Is there any task you've been meaning to get to and keep putting off, or that you routinely delay doing? Which of these factors applies to your procrastination tendencies? In your journal, write down any ways in which you've been procrastinating and what seems to drive it.

Is Procrastination Always a Bad Thing?

Some researchers have suggested that procrastination's benefits should not be overlooked. For example, procrastinating gives us longer to come up with solutions, and can also allow us to harness the pressure of a deadline to energize our efforts.

Management professor Adam Grant cited the benefits of procrastination on creativity in his writings. According to Dr. Grant, our initial ideas tend to be more traditional. Giving ourselves additional time can lead to more innovative solutions, which we never reach if we finish the task as soon as possible.

These potential advantages need to be weighed against the stress, missed deadlines, and lower quality work linked to procrastinating.

Strategies for Beating Procrastination

Understanding what causes procrastination gives us clues as to how to break out of it. Because multiple factors lead to procrastination, we need a wide range of tools to choose from to overcome it. These tools can be divided into three domains:

- Think (cognitive)
- Act (behavioral)
- Be (mindfulness)

Over time, you can find a set of strategies from these three areas that work well for you.

Some conditions can make procrastination mostly likely. Depression saps our energy and motivation, making it hard to take care of things. Individuals with ADHD struggle to meet deadlines due to difficulty focusing on a task and low motivation to complete it.

Anxiety disorders can also lead to procrastination — for example, and a person might delay writing an e-mail due to fear of saying something stupid.

Think: Cognitive Strategies

Much of our procrastination comes from how we think about the task and our willingness and ability to complete it. Strategic changes in our thinking can weaken procrastination's pull.

Acknowledge that You Probably Won't Feel like Doing It Sooner, either

We might assume we'll get to a task once we feel like doing it. Though, the truth is that we probably won't want to do it after any more than we want to do it now. We can stop waiting for a magical time down the road when it's effortless to do the task.

Challenge Beliefs about Having to Do Something "Perfectly"

We often put off starting a task because we've set unrealistically high standards for how well we must do it.

Keep in mind that it doesn't have to be perfect; it just needs to be done.

Choose the Think strategies that resonate with you and write them in your journal to practice when needed.

Being on Time

Being late reflects a specific type of procrastination, namely a delay in moving ourselves from one place to another by a deadline. Follow these principles if you want to improve your punctuality:

Be realistic about the time required. Time how long it takes to reach your destination. Be sure to factor in time for incidentals like saying goodbye to your family and giving yourself a buffer for the unexpected (e.g., traffic delays) so you don't underestimate the actual time required.

Be careful about setting your clock or watch ahead to help you be on time. This strategy often backfires because we know our watch is fast, and we can disregard it altogether.

Avoid starting an activity close to time to leave. Beware of trying to squeeze in one more activity before leaving for your destination, even if you think it will take "just a minute." There's a good chance it will take more time than you have and end up making you late.

Bring things to do in case you're early. If you're afraid of being early and then wasting time with nothing to do, bring a journal or some other enjoyable or productive way to pass the time if you're early.

CHAPTER 7:

Using CBT to Overcome Jealousy

Ending jealousy is like altering every mental or behavioral response. It begins with consciousness. Awareness lets you see that the predicted stories are not real in your head. If you are so straightforward, you no longer respond to the possibilities your imagination might imagine. Jealousy and anger are emotional reactions that are not true in believing situations in your head. You should change what you think affects what your imagination projects and remove these harmful emotional reactions. Even if the reaction is warranted, envy and rage are not good ways to cope with the situation and get what we want. Trying to change anxiety or resentment when you feel like trying to control a car skidding on ice. Your ability to deal with the situation is much improved if you can clear the risk before we get there. This means addressing the beliefs that cause jealousy rather than trying to control your emotions.

Dissolving relationships permanently means changing the underlying beliefs of fear and unconscious expectations of what the partner is doing.

The Steps to end jealous Reactions Permanently Are

a. Recover personal power so that you can control your emotions and stop reactive behavior.

b. Identify the core convictions that trigger the emotional response.

c. Be mindful that your convictions are not valid. This is distinct from scientifically "knowing" that the claims are not real.

d. Gain power over your focus so that you can actively select your mind's story and emotions.

Several factors establish the envy dynamic. Practical solutions will tackle multiple elements of values, experiences, feelings, and strength of personal will. You will leave the doors open to those negative emotions and behaviors if you lack one or more of these components.

You can step back from the story by practicing some simple exercises and refrain from the emotional reaction. You can do it if you want to change your feelings and actions. It only takes the readiness to acquire adequate skills.

Principle Triggers of Jealousy Are Convictions Which Create Insecurity Feelings

Low self-esteem is based on convictions of who we are. To eradicate fear and low self-esteem, we do not have to change our confidence in the false self-image. While some people believe this may be difficult, it's only tricky because most people haven't learned the skills needed to change their faith.

When you practice your skills, it takes minimal effort to change a belief. You just stop thinking about the story. It takes more effort than it does to believe something.

Self-Judgment May Intensify the Feeling of Insecurity

It is not enough to "learn" the emotion intellectually. Only in this way will the Inner Judge abuse us with criticism of what we do. The Interior Judge could use this knowledge to push us into more vulnerability by an emotional downward spiral. You will need to develop skills to dissolve beliefs and falsified self-images and to control your mind projects. The practices and skills of the audio sessions are available. The first and second sessions are free and should give us an idea of how the mind works to create emotions. Sessions 1 and 2 also give you great exercises to regain some personal power and adjust your emotions.

One of the steps to changing behavior is to see how we create the emotion of wrath or jealousy from our minds. This very step will allow us to take responsibility and puts us in a position to change our emotions.

We don't take responsibility if you're in a relationship with a jealous partner and want to change your behavior to avoid envy. Saying things like, "when you wouldn't, then I wouldn't react like this." This kind of language flags a powerless attitude and attempts to control your behavior by dealing with it.

How the Mind Produces the Emotions of Anger and Jealousy?

I described in the description below the mechanism of jealousy and anger. When you try to overcome envy, you probably already know the complexities I explain. This explanation can help to fill the holes in how the mind turns knowledge into self-judgment and increases low self-esteem and insecurity. This theoretical understanding will contribute to the development of consciousness to see these complexities when you do so. But you need a different set of skills to make significant changes. You don't have enough details about how you build your emotional reactions. Just like realizing you have a flat tire; you didn't know how to patch the tire because you stumbled over the screw. I will use a guy as a jealous companion for the example. I am talking about different pictures in mind, and you can refer to the chart below or see the Relationship Matrix for a more detailed description of these images.

Compensating for Fear

To overcome the emotion created from the hidden false image, he concentrates on his perceived positive qualities to counteract the emotion created by his secret image. The man creates a more optimistic False Image of himself from these attributes. I call this the Projected Picture because he needs to be seen like this. The mental consequence of a positive self-image is not self-rejection or indignity. There is greater acceptance, and he generates more love and happiness. Notice that he has not changed; depending on the moment, he only has a different image in his mind.

The hidden image belief causes unhappiness, while the projected image causes more pleasant emotions. It must be remembered that both pictures are fake. Both images are in the mind of the man, and nobody is him. He is the one who creates and reacts in his imagination to the images. In his imagination, he's not an image.

The mind of the man blends the projected image with the qualities attracted by women. The characteristics are often considered positive because women are attracted to them.

When a man receives attention from a woman, he links himself to the projected image instead of "not good enough." The increased trust in the projected image leads to more social acceptance, love, and happiness.

CHAPTER 8:

Using CBT to Beat Addiction

A mind that has been ruined by drug addiction is the perfect breeding ground for negative thoughts and other emotional health issues. Managing challenging thoughts and emotions is hard enough for a sober person, but the experience is ten times worse when you consider a drug addict. Thankfully, drug addicts can benefit from CBT. Cognitive-behavioral therapy has been shown to achieve long-lasting results in the treatment of various addiction types.

The Following Are some of the Benefits of CBT in Addiction Treatment

• **Provides a Network of Support**

Cognitive-behavioral therapy allows addicts to have a network of support, which is very crucial during the recovery phase. The average addict, if not given positive encouragement, could easily relapse into drug abuse. Therapists are there to offer positive encouragement and gently guide these people toward full healing. When addicts realize that no one cares about them, they are likely to go back to seek solace from drugs. Having a network of support is critical for avoiding relapse and ensuring general emotional well-being. People are social beings. Thanks to the support network, addicts have someone to talk to.

- **Increased positive Thought Patterns**

Addicts often struggle with a negative thought pattern that makes them feel helpless, ultimately making them go back to doing drugs. An addict struggles with many bleak thoughts and feelings. However, through the power of positivity, they can overcome their mental and emotional health issues. CBT emphasizes positivity. The more positive an individual is, the less likely they are to slide back into drug addiction. Therapists help addicts overcome their conditions by planting positive thoughts in their subconscious. This helps addicts become positive by default. And whenever they experience emotional troubles, they have someone to guide them.

- **Enhancement of Self-Esteem**

Low self-esteem is one of the reasons why people turn to drugs and alcohol. They want to forget their misery and helplessness. But cognitive behavioral therapy helps addicts develop a great self-image. As their self-esteem level goes up, they find less desire to escape reality through drugs and alcohol. They are happy to be themselves. Therapists constantly reinforce addicts' self-esteem and thus raise their desire of wanting a better life than the one they presently have. To get rid of an addiction, the affected person must want to change their circumstances, and this desire becomes natural when an addict's self-esteem is given a boost.

- **Learning to Resist Peer Pressure**

Since we are social beings seeking peer acceptance, it is exceptionally challenging to resist peer pressure. It is challenging for the average person, and ten times more challenging for the drug addict. Cognitive-behavioral therapy equips addicts with the skills for overcoming peer pressure and focusing on their important life goals. When it comes to resisting peer pressure, they are trained first to imagine saying "no" to their peers, and then actually saying "no" within a controlled environment. By the end of the training, they won't have any difficulty saying "no" to both their peers and anyone else who might negatively influence.

- **Cost-Effectiveness**

Cognitive-behavioral therapy is one of the most affordable addiction treatment methods. Some other treatment methods, like rehabs, have in-house arrangements for the patient. These treatment methods can be incredibly expensive.

Cognitive-behavioral therapy can be conducted on an outpatient basis and achieve great results. Insurance plans even cover this treatment method. Cognitive-behavioral therapy is not one-sided. For its success, both the therapist and the patient must work side by side. If the patient is not cooperative, then the treatment will tumble down. Cognitive-behavioral therapy is not complicated. It involves general procedures that lead to the restoration of health. There are no expensive or complicated tools required.

- **Gradual Steps**

Overcoming an addiction is no walk in the park. It is a time-consuming quest. Remedies that claim to offer instant results are misleading. In cognitive-behavioral therapy, a therapist introduces new principles to the patient as they advance through the treatment. There are principles set aside for the beginners and principles set aside for those who have reached the advanced stage. Walking through these steps, the patient's resolve is strengthened, and they are less likely to run back to drugs or alcohol than patients who have been through any other treatment model. The beauty of cognitive behavioral therapy is that it doesn't advertise itself as a quick fix. It takes real effort to achieve results. However, the effects are long-lasting.

- **Continuity of normal Activities**

Cognitive-behavioral therapy is done on an outpatient arrangement. The patient is free to indulge in other activities for the rest of their time. This is unlike rehabs, where patients are held on campus, effectively suspending their daily engagements such as going to work. With cognitive behavioral therapy, patients are neither separated from their family nor do they have to seek leave. Because of its flexibility, more people are willing to take this treatment method. And if the sessions are scheduled at night, then your day will run without even a slight hitch.

- **Gradual end to Therapy**

Cognitive-behavioral therapy places the entire focus on the patient. The concepts and exercises may be adjusted following how the patient is faring. In some forms of addiction therapy, the treatment lasts only for a specific time, and then it is cut off. This kind of arrangement doesn't take care of patients who would take ordinarily long to recover fully. In cognitive-behavioral therapy, the first few weeks are typically intensive. Still, as the patient's condition improves, the therapist finds less need to have intensive sessions and focuses on the patient's recovery speed.

CHAPTER 9:

Using CBT to Overcome Regret and Guilt

D o you ruminate about the mistakes you've made? Do you want to feel more comfortable with your past choices?

How Do You Feel about Guilt?

Everyone makes mistakes. We all have our faults. Even the kindest, most patient, and most moral of us have made poor choices. Unfortunately, hurting other people is part of being human.

CBT gives you the tools to understand where guilt and regret come from, how to move past them, and how to avoid making bad choices in the future. Remember, how you react to events – including your mistakes – is just as important as the event itself.

You Are Not responsible for Everything

If you are prone to guilt and regret, you probably have a habit of assuming too much responsibility. When you are too quick to say, "Yes, this situation is entirely my fault!" your view becomes warped. In reality, most unfortunate events aren't caused by one person. Life is more complicated than that.

For example, let's say that your relationship has recently broken down. You and your partner have fallen into a pattern of getting into trivial fights that turn into screaming matches. To make matters worse, you disagree on a couple of other issues, including the question of marriage — you want to marry, and they don't.

So, who is at fault in this story? If it happened to a friend, you would probably reassure them that there are many play factors.

Slicing the Responsibility Pie

The following exercise will help you step back from a problem or situation and understand the part you played in it.

Exercise: The Responsibility Pie

Make a list of everyone who played a role in the event you're feeling wrong about, such as a breakup or a fight.

Now, draw a large circle on a piece of paper. This is your Responsibility, Pie. Draw lines to divide this pie up into slices. Draw a slice for everyone on your list. Make the size of the pieces proportionate to their responsibility. Don't worry about getting the sizes or percentages exact. Go with your gut instinct.

Yes, but what if It Was My Fault?

Of course, you might have made a big mistake, and no one else is to blame.

For instance, let's say you go to a conference for work, get drunk, and cheat on your partner with a colleague who doesn't know you aren't single. Your partner finds out, and they end the relationship.

In this case, your partner isn't to blame. If you were to create a Responsibility Pie, the only name on there would be yours.

Exercise: What Are Your Beliefs About Guilt?

Complete the sentences below:

- "If I didn't feel guilty, I would…"
- "I don't think I can give up my feelings of guilt because…"

- "Guilt is useful because…"

What do you think your answers reveal about your beliefs?

Common Beliefs about Guilt & Why They Are So destructive

1. **"If I Feel Guilty, I Must Have Something to Feel Guilty about."**

   This is simply untrue. For instance, some people feel guilty when they survive an accident in which others died. This kind of "survivor guilt" is irrational. It's an example of emotional reasoning. Just because you think you are a terrible person who should be ashamed of yourself doesn't mean you have anything to feel wrong about. Only by stepping back and taking a long look at the situation can you come to a reasonable conclusion.

2. **"If I Feel Guilty, It Means I Am a bad Person."**

   Even if most people would agree that your guilt is justified, you are not the wrong person. This line of thinking is an example of generalization, which is a cognitive distortion.

Like everyone else, you are a complex individual who has done great things and made mistakes.

3. **"Guilt Will Stop Me from Hurting People in the Future."**

Don't fall into the trap of assuming that guilt somehow protects you from repeating your mistakes.

You might think, "Well, at least holding onto my guilt will make me think twice before doing something wrong!"

This approach is doomed to fail because it undermines your self-confidence. Your morals and values are better at helping you make good choices, not guilt.

Guilt also damages your relationships with other people. It makes you averse and afraid, and your loved ones will always have the sense that your decisions and emotions are driven by something they can't see or understand.

4. **"I Need to Feel Guilty Forever because I Need to Punish Myself for what I've Done."**

In small doses, guilt is healthy. It's a kind of warning signal. Guilt lets you know that you've violated your moral code. When we feel guilty, we know it's time to make amends and apologize if appropriate.

Guilt becomes self-indulgent after a while. It doesn't always feel like a punishment. It can become almost comfortable. If you don't let go of your guilt, you'll build a self-image as a "bad person." You need to take responsibility for your past and how your feelings keep you stuck in place.

5. **"If I Let Myself Stop Feeling Guilty, this Means I Approve of My Actions."**

Have you ever been reluctant to forgive someone because you don't want them to let them off the hook? The same principle can apply to your guilt.

On some level, you might think that allowing yourself to live guilt-free means that you are magnificent with the things you've done.

6. "If I Make a Mistake, I Am an unacceptable human Being."

This thought can be traced back to a single core belief: "I must be perfect, or I am worthless." This belief is both illogical and harmful. No one is perfect.

The sooner you realize this, the happier you will be. You wouldn't expect your friends and family to behave impeccably at all times, would you?

7. "If I Keep Analyzing the Situation long enough, I Can Work Out Exactly How Much of the Blame I Deserve."

Some of us want to know precisely what went wrong in a situation that left us feeling guilty. Unfortunately, the world doesn't work like that.

There's no objective, scientific way to figure out exactly how much blame lies with us in most cases. It's smarter to invest your energy looking forward instead.

CHAPTER 10:

CBT and Mindfulness

As you can imagine, embracing positivity in everyday life can make a profound change in how happy and peaceful your overall life is. When you utilize a positive mindset every day, you will find that life, in general, tends to flow and unfold with more ease and that people in your life then start to respond to you in more optimistic ways.

While motivating yourself to maintain positivity every day is not easy, it is more than possible and certainly worth the effort.

First, positive people are almost always positive, no matter what, because of two key things:

They practice being optimistic about strengthening this capability further.

They choose to be positive because it feels a heck of a lot better than drowning in a pool of negativity.

We are not born positive or negative, and one person is not more capable of optimism from the other. Stop making excuses about your skills, challenges, or situations you are enduring regarding your level of optimism. There are no aspects that make positivity easy, even though many see it this way.

Positivity is primarily a choice. It would be best to have both free will and awareness to succeed and maintain a good sense of optimism in your life. Guess what? Every person, even you, is wired with free will and conscious awareness! You are always in the right place to be more positive and start reaping the benefits from it.

When you are aware of yourself and your life, you will then notice when you are starting to venture down the path of negativity. Having this awareness jumpstarts the choice between optimism and pessimism. Below are some terrific tips you can begin to practice to gain optimum results!

Mindfulness-based Cognitive Therapy focuses on cognitive therapy and mindfulness, rather than behavioral aspects from CBT. It looks at attitudes and mood, which is why it works well for people who find themselves in severe depressive states and suffer from unhappiness regularly. Breathing and meditation is a critical component of this therapy.

Mindfulness is about self-awareness in the same way that CBT is. Although CBT is hugely tailored around mindfulness, it involves analyzing and working on those things, which sometimes means we judge our thoughts and feelings. CBT also focuses on the behavior aspect and evokes change, whereas mindfulness raises awareness and believes that becoming aware can change without forcing it. Both concepts focus on the present and try to implement changes moving forward.

By adding mindfulness to cognitive therapy, we appreciate ourselves and show flexibility in our thoughts. There is growing evidence suggesting that MBCT can be a beneficial treatment for mental health issues, and it's often thought of being a great self-help tool (Edelman, 2006).

Important Ideas in Mindfulness-based cognitive Therapy

Mindfulness-based Cognitive Therapy focuses on emotions, thoughts, and attitudes. Basic ideas about MBCT are:

- It is building up a tolerance or coping mechanism that allows us to deal with painful situations better.
- I am open and non-judgmental.
- You are reaching an enhanced state of awareness.
- It is allowing us to gain insight into ourselves and being in touch with how we feel.
- Using meditation techniques to reflect, recover, and cope with specific situations. This can promote emotional wellness.
- We are incorporating breathing techniques to help us calm down and cope with our feelings and emotions.

Mindfulness-based Cognitive Therapy is aimed at those who suffer from heightened depression regularly.

Its key components teach clients to break from those negative thought patterns and cope better while improving self-awareness.

How Does MBCT Work?

MBCT aims to try and prevent relapses of depression. If a person suffers from regular depressive episodes, it's essential to try and change this pattern. MBCT focuses on changing your relationship with your emotions. Mindfulness activities, such as meditation, can help to create balance and just like CBT.

You can start to change your automatic negative thought patterns and replace them with new ones.

MBCT is about creating a routine and adopting mindfulness techniques to cope with an overwhelming situation. The hope is that you can replace your negative thought patterns and prevent those feelings of sadness from turning into depression (Psychology Today, 2019).

Problems that May Be addressed by MBCT

Much like CBT, mindfulness-based cognitive therapy is mainly used when treating depression, including moods and feelings of sadness. It has been recognized to help those suffering from anxiety disorders, relationship issues, pain, stress, and substance misuse. Let's not forget how useful these coping strategies are with panic too.

If you start to feel down, overwhelmed, or feel a panic attack coming on, the techniques involved in this treatment can prevent it from escalating into depression. However, this type of therapy is usually suggested under a therapist if you suffer from depressive episodes regularly (usually three episodes or more).

MBCT Techniques and Exercises

Below are some different techniques and exercises that you might want to explore as part of your MBCT routine. Remember, the routine is everything, so planning in time to breathe, meditate, or exercise is a great way to start your MBCT treatment.

- Breathing Exercises — Before you can meditate, you need to master your breathing. When we breathe, we typically use our chest, and we raise it and down as we inhale and exhale. Breathing from the diaphragm and stomach area is recommended with MBCT, which involves relaxing your stomach and allowing it to rise and fall as you breathe deeply. You may need to practice breathing daily, so spend some quiet time focusing on your breathing technique. You can lay back in the chair, close or open your eyes, or you may prefer to lie down.

- Guided Meditations — Many people learn to get themselves into a meditative state without being guided. Still, for beginners, there are many guided meditations you can use online, on channels like YouTube. Often, guided meditations focus on a specific area, but there are ones that focus on sadness and depression. If you're going to try a guided meditation, research the different ones available and listen to them for a few seconds until you find a soothing voice. Once you've found the one for you, kick back and relax. You should practice your breathing techniques for a couple of minutes, just before you begin.

- Walking Meditation — With any meditation, you need something to focus on, and in this case, you focus on your walking. You don't focus on each step or look at your feet, and you focus on the fact that you are walking. Walking is a great way to clear your mind, and because it's exercise, it allows you to refocus, and you will feel refreshed.

- Yoga Stretches — Yoga is an excellent exercise for mindfulness, CBT, and MBCT, as it is already a meditative exercise. There are different types of yoga, and some are more spiritual than others. Kundalini Yoga is meditation-based and involves quite a lot of breathing exercises as well as chanting. You can attend a class, or there are tutorials online, too, if you would prefer.

Other techniques from CBT, like journaling, are helpful for MBCT. Recording your thoughts shows that you're paying attention to yourself and your needs. It's a form of self-care which we could all do with a little more of.

MBCT is focused a lot more on positivity, so you could also think of daily things you are thankful for (Edelman, 2006).

Benefits of Mindfulness

As mentioned already, being mindful is a way to take care of yourself, and this has numerous benefits for your mind and body. This includes:

- Better general health and state of mind.
- Improved concentration levels.
- Insight into one's self and more in tune with emotions.
- Better control of thoughts and the ability to reason.
- Stronger problem-solving skills.
- Feeling motivated and positive.
- Decreased stress and anxiety.

Mindfulness Skills

Being mindful helps us to embed many skills that can help us in our life. It can help us process our thoughts more positively, as maintaining a fit and healthy outlook. As we feel happier and healthier, we take back control of our lives and are less likely to feel depressed, anxious, or stressed.

Mindfulness can help us to appreciate ourselves and understand the importance of caring for our mind and body. When we feel motivated and content, we can overcome barriers that hold us back. We can also feel rested and relaxed, which helps us to reason.

This means that we often live for the moment and live a happy, fulfilling life!

Conclusion

I ndeed, CBT starts with a relatively straightforward way to understand a challenging situation and how we react to it. You have to remember that cognitive-behavioral therapy focuses on the three major components of a psychological problem: thoughts, emotions, and behaviors.

This simply means that when you experience a challenging situation, it is essential that you break it down into these components. When you break it down in this manner, you gain clarity about where to intervene and how to do it. In other words, if there is a chain of reactions of both behavior and emotional feelings that arise from having a particular negative thought, the best approach is to go back into reexamining the thought. However, if a negative behavior pattern seems to be the main problem, the wiser thing to do is learn a new response to the situation.

The truth is, there is no quicker way to fix your anxiety. It takes time and commitment for you to overcome your fears fully. When you go through cognitive behavioral therapy, it is essential that you face your fears head-on rather than trying to run away from them. This might make you feel worse at first, but it is only after that you can start feeling better. The most important thing is for you to try as much as you can to stick to your therapy and the advice given by your therapist.

Your pace or recovery may be slow, and this can be discouraging at the time, but you have to remember that it will be useful in the long-run. Therefore, rather than giving up, keep pressing on, and you will eventually reap the benefits. To support your therapy, you must start making positive choices. This includes everything from your level of activity to your social life and how that affects your condition. The best route is for you to begin by setting goals and making informed decisions that will boost your relaxation and functionality levels and offer you a positive mental outlook in your daily life.

Take time to learn about your anxiety so that it becomes easier to overcome it. Education is essential in ensuring that you know what it takes to get to the other recovery side. Right, that alone will not cure your condition, but it will help you make sense of your healing therapy.

Cultivate your support network to be isolated and lonely, as loneliness can make your anxiety even worse. When you establish a robust system of support from your therapist, family, and friends, you will significantly lower your vulnerability level. Make a point to see your support group frequently so that you can share with them your worries, concerns, and progress.

Also, remember to adopt a healthy lifestyle by engaging in physical activities and eating healthy foods. This regimen goes a long way in helping to achieve relaxation by relieving tension and anxiety. Therefore, in your daily routine, make it a point to schedule regular exercises. Also, refrain from foods and drinks that may make your anxiety worse, such as those containing caffeine or alcohol.

Printed in Great Britain
by Amazon

55322243R00050